CONRAD K. BUTLER

The passenger jets of the world for kids

The importance of air transport in the development of today's world is undeniable. For example, it is estimated that in 2019 alone, planes carried over 4.5 billion passengers. Aviation is not only a means of transport, it is also a huge branch of industry, technology, and science and one of the driving forces of our civilization. It is therefore worth taking a look at the machines that had an above-average impact on the history and shape of the aviation market as we know it today.

Airbus A300

The list opens with the first aircraft created by the Airbus consortium: the wide-body, twin-engine Airbus A300. Airbus sealed its debut with the opening of a new page in the history of aviation: the A300 was the first wide-body aircraft with two engines (until then, this category was reserved only for aircraft with three or four engines).

This plane was a specific response to the needs of airlines, which in the face of the fuel crisis of that time needed a cheaper, two-engine long-range jet. During the 36 years of production of the A300 model, more than 560 copies of this aircraft were made. Many of them still fly today.

IranAir
EP-IBD
A300

Airbus A380

The presence of the Airbus A380 is indisputable. It is currently the largest machine used to transport passengers in the world. This giant appeared on the market in the middle of 2005. The A380 has become a legend almost like the Boeing 747. In many respects, it even beat the famous Jumbo Jet: it takes on its board (or the decks, because the A380 consists of two levels) even 853 passengers, and its take-off weight is up to 590 tons. However, this is only the tip of the iceberg, because the A380 holds a lot of aviation records. We believe that in the long run, the A380 will become a legend like the Jumbo Jet.

EXPO 2020 DUBAI UAE
Emirates
الإمارات

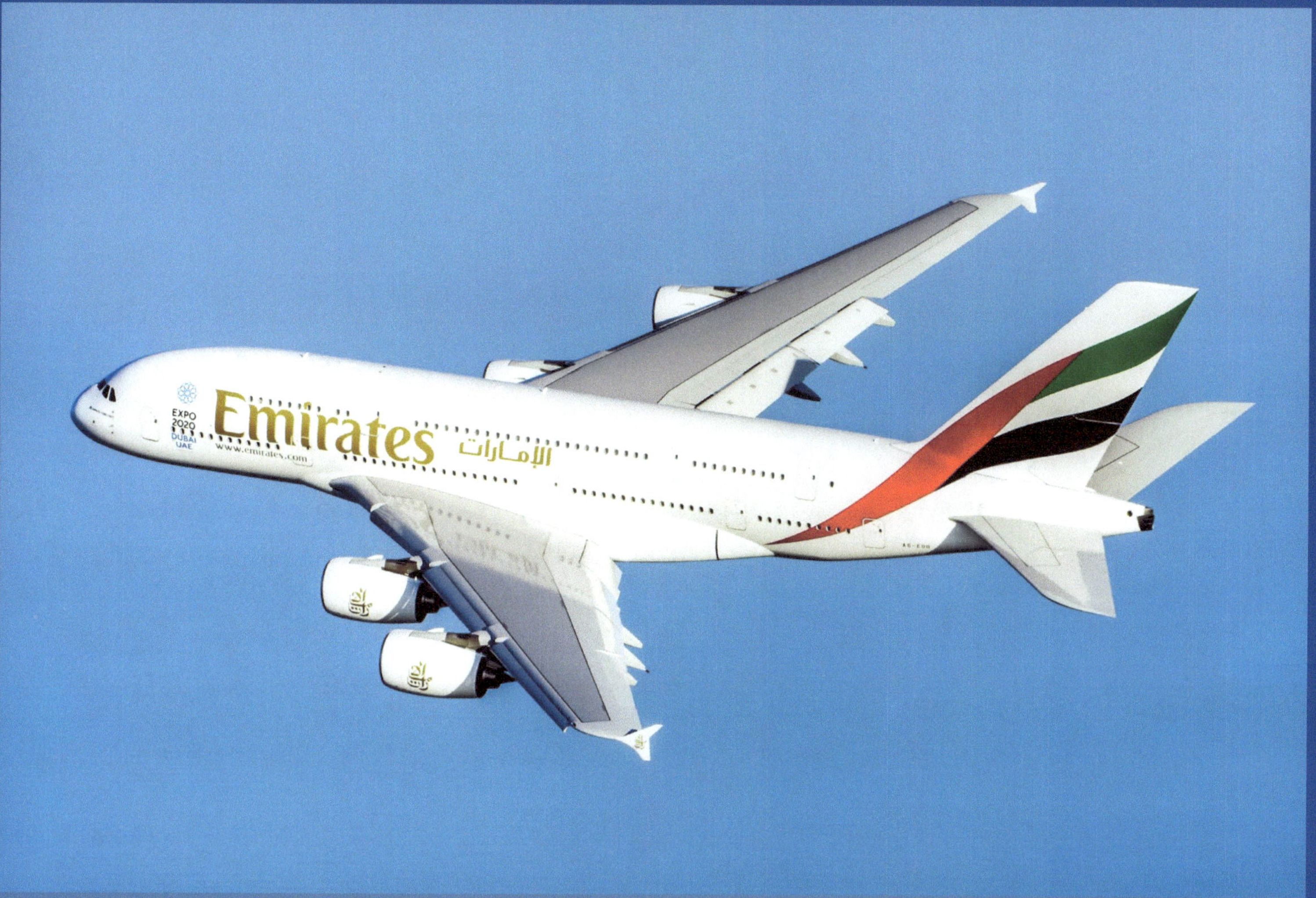

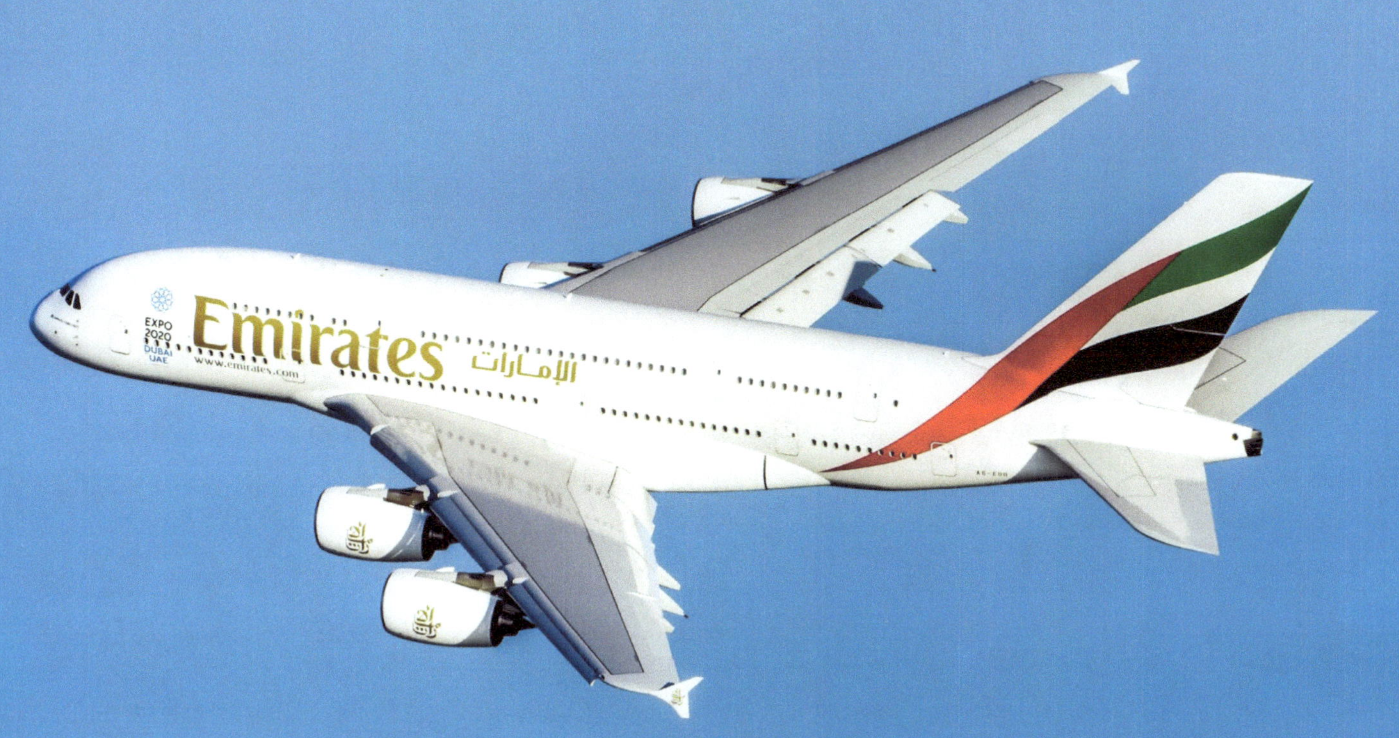

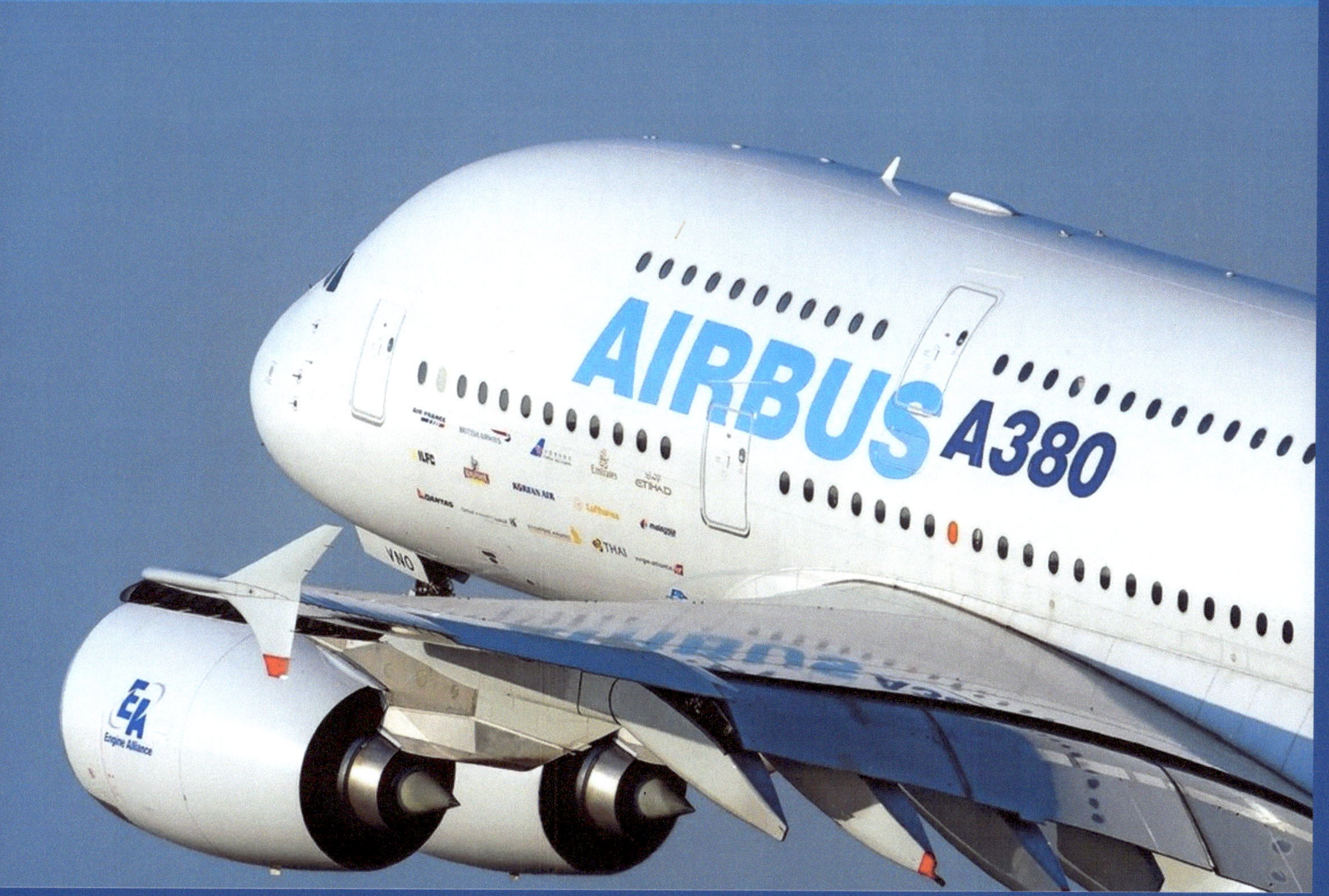
AIRBUS A380

Boeing 777

The Boeing 777 is currently the largest twin-engine aircraft. It has been produced continuously since 1993 and it has come down the assembly lines in the number of more than 1,600 copies. For the needs of this giant, the largest and most powerful engine used in civil aviation was created: General Electric GE90 with a thrust of up to 514 kN and a diameter of 3.53 meters in the housing (that's more than the diameter of the entire Boeing 737 fuselage!). The importance of this aircraft is often underestimated. Boeing proved with it that twin-engine machines, much cheaper in operation, can achieve record ranges, carrying a similar number of passengers to that which can be carried by planes equipped with four engines.

Concorde

Concorde is undoubtedly one of the aviation icons after the Second World War. This plane is the fruit of a collaboration between British and French engineers. Their work is the realization of dreams of rapid movement between continents. To do this, it was necessary to exceed the speed of sound. Overcoming the phenomena accompanying the wave crisis, however, required the design of an airframe very resistant to high temperatures and powerful engines consuming huge amounts of fuel. This made the Concorde tremendously expensive and its operating costs very high. If we add that about a hundred passengers could have boarded it ... The concept of building a Concorde-like airplane still sits in the minds of the largest aviation manufacturers. Designers of the greatest powers of the aviation industry are preparing concepts of aircraft that are equally fast, but much cheaper to operate. Perhaps soon we will again be able to exceed the speed of sound on board a passenger plane.

Boeing 707

This plane is the first passenger jet to achieve real commercial success. It is thanks to this machine that Boeing has become a world leader, pushing its rivals Lockheed and Douglas off its pedestal. The Boeing 707 became the plane that was intended to be the first liner jet: the De Havilland Comet. The Boeing 707 made its first flight in 1954, and it was produced until the end of the 1970s. During this time, just over 1,000 of these aircraft left the production lines. Dozens of them still fly today!

De Havilland Comet

The De Havilland Comet is a unique plane. It is the first passenger jet used by airlines around the world. Despite many pioneering solutions, it did not achieve great success in the market. This was mainly due to the problems that plagued the structure: construction and design flaws, which resulted in at least a few catastrophes. Only subsequent versions of the Comet became the jets that more and more customers began to rely on. But it was too late: a rival from Seattle was lurking around the corner with an ace up his sleeve, the Boeing 707. The Comet was produced in 125 copies. It was a four-engine machine with a range of up to 5,200 kilometers, capable of reaching a record level of 12 kilometers and speeds of up to 840 kilometers per hour. The plane took up to 81 passengers on board. To this day, no Comet has survived: it can only be admired in museums.

Boeing 747 "Jumbo Jet"

The Boeing 747 is one of the most popular aircraft in the world. The machine with a distinctive hump is the first wide-body plane in the world. It is an icon of the American era of the "American dream" – the 747 allowed us to achieve more and better. It takes up to 600 passengers on board and enables a flight of up to 14,000 kilometers without refueling. These opportunities have convinced not only hundreds of airlines around the world. Although from a technical point of view, the Jumbo Jet was not a big step forward, its symbolism, popularity, and low operating costs contributed to the popularization of air transport.

BRITISH AIRWAYS

The 'family' of the Airbus A320

Another point on our list is the Airbus A320 family of planes. Launched in the late 1980s, the series of planes stood in the shadow of the famous Boeing 737 for almost 30 years. Today, the A320 family is just as important for world transport as the aforementioned 737. This is evidenced by the records of orders and sales of these machines. To date, more than 9,000 have been delivered, and thousands more are waiting for their place on the production line. The A320 series is also important for another reason. It is a small technological "revolution" that took place with the introduction of the first machine of this type to the market.

Boeing 737

If you flew somewhere by plane, the probability is high that it was a Boeing 737. Over the 50 years of its production, more than ten thousand of these machines have been produced and since then they have carried over 10 billion passengers and millions of tons of cargo, and during that time they were full time consistently developed. It is thanks to the creation of the 737 that the importance of air transport has grown so much since the 1970s. The Boeing 737 is a narrow-body aircraft used to carry passengers over short and medium distances. Its project was created in the 1960s in the USA, as a response to the growing demand of American passengers for fast travel over a distance of several thousand kilometers. It quickly turned out that this way of traveling was appreciated not only in the United States but also in the rest of the world.

Lockheed L-1011 TriStar

The L-1011 TriStar is a solid piece of aviation history because the long-range aircraft produced by Lockheed Martin was at the time of its premiere the most technically advanced passenger machine in the world. But the competition from the Boeing 747 or McDonnell Douglas DC-10 turned out to be too strong and the Lockheed Martin L-1011 TriStar did not gain much popularity. The company produced 250 units of this model, but it was also its first and last civilian airliner, which ultimately caused $ 2.5 billion in losses.

Check also:

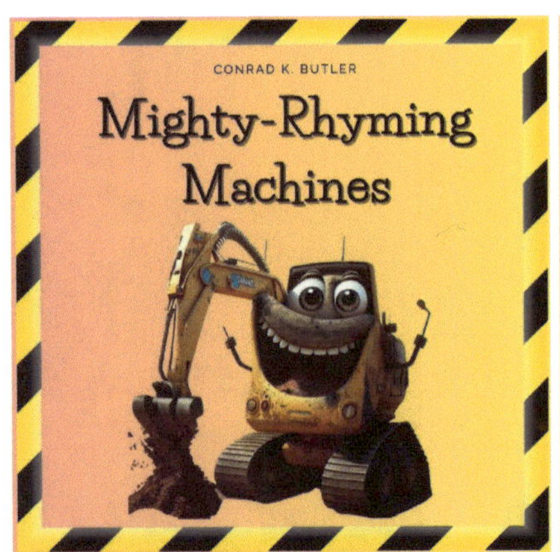

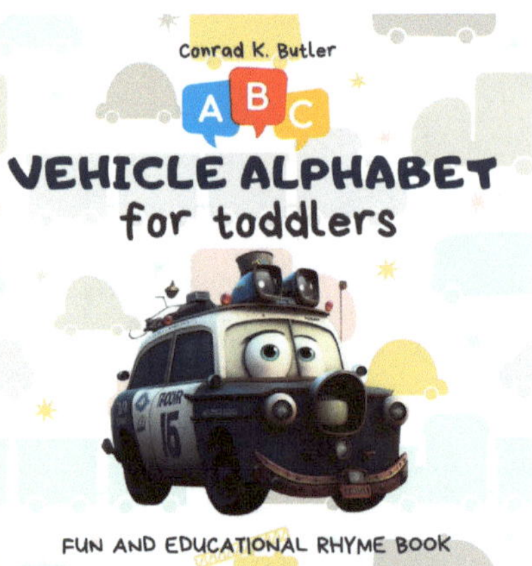

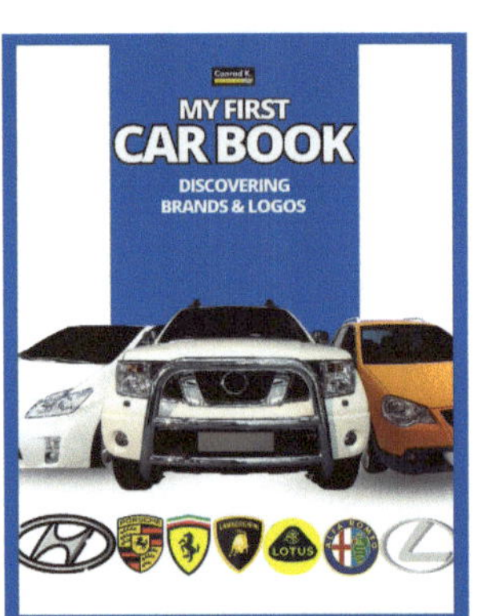

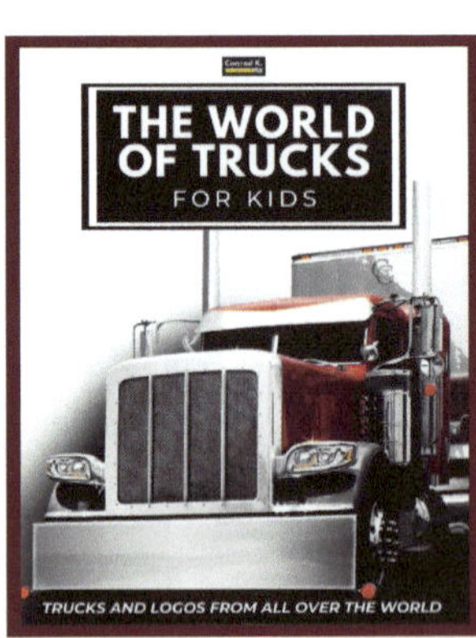

and much more!